Runners:
Bed & Tabletop

LEISURE ARTS, INC. • Maumelle, Arkansas

EDITORIAL STAFF

Senior Product Director: Pam Stebbins

Creative Art Director: Katherine Laughlin

Publications Director: Leah Lampirez

Technical Editors: Lisa Lancaster and Jean Lewis

Editorial Writer: Susan Frantz Wiles

Art Category Manager: Lora Puls

Graphic Artist: Jessica Bramlett

Prepress Technician: Stephanie Johnson

Contributing Photographer: Jason Masters

Contributing Photo Stylist: Lori Wenger

BUSINESS STAFF

President and Chief Executive Officer: Fred F. Pruss

Senior Vice President of Operations: Jim Dittrich

Vice President of Retail Sales: Martha Adams

Chief Financial Officer: Tiffany P. Childers

Controller: Teresa Eby

Information Technology Director: Brian Roden

Director of E-Commerce: Mark Hawkins

Manager of E-Commerce: Robert Young

ISBN-13/EAN: 978-1-4647-3536-3

UPC: 0-28906-06480-3

For Sue Marsh of Whistlepig Creek Productions, bags and "smallish quilts" are the kind of projects that drive her passion. Sewing from the age of 12, she has loved quick projects since the beginning. "I did my first quilt project from a Quilt in a Day book. I literally made a king-size quilt in a day, and I was hooked." Sue pursued quilting as a hobby while working in the petroleum industry for 15 years. Then in 1997, she turned to full-time designing of quilt projects and fabrics. For more about Sue and Whistlepig Creek Productions, visit her pages on Facebook, Pinterest, and wpcreek.blogspot.com.

Contents

Beautify your home with quick and easy quilted runners for beds and tabletops — or hang them on the wall! Some have matching pillow shams and other accessories.

Top It Off Bed Runner

Finished Bed Runner Size: 87" x 27" (221 cm x 69 cm)
Finished Block Size: 12^1/$_2$" x 17" (32 cm x 43 cm)

SHOPPING LIST

Yardage is based on 43"/44" (109 cm/112 cm) wide fabric with a usable width of 40" (102 cm).

☐ 1 yd (91 cm) of black and white print fabric

☐ ^{1}/$_4$ yd (23 cm) of grey tone-on-tone fabric

☐ 1^3/$_8$ yds (1.3 m) of solid white fabric

☐ ^{3}/$_4$ yd (69 cm) of solid black fabric

☐ 2^3/$_4$ yds (2.5 m) of fabric for backing

☐ ^{1}/$_2$ yd (46 cm) of fabric for binding

☐ 35" x 95" (89 cm x 241 cm) piece of batting

CUTTING THE PIECES

*Follow **Rotary Cutting**, page 42, to cut fabric. Cut all strips from the selvage-to-selvage width of the fabric. All measurements include ^{1}/$_4$" seam allowances.*

From black and white print fabric:

- Cut 1 strip 8^1/$_2$" wide. From this strip, cut 6 **rectangle A's** 6" x 8^1/$_2$".
- Cut 6 **outer borders** 3^1/$_2$" wide.

From grey tone-on-tone print fabric:

- Cut 1 strip 1^1/$_2$" wide. From this strip, cut 2 **strip A's** 1^1/$_2$" x 20".
- Cut 2 strips 2" wide. From these strips, cut 2 **strip B's** 2" x 26".
- Cut 1 strip 2^1/$_2$" wide. From this strip, cut 2 **strip C's** 2^1/$_2$" x 20".

From solid white fabric:

- Cut 1 strip 8^1/$_2$" wide. From this strip, cut 1 **rectangle B** 8^1/$_2$" x 20".
- Cut 2 strips 1^1/$_2$" wide. From these strips, cut 12 **strip D's** 1^1/$_2$" x 6".
- Cut 1 strip 11" wide. From this strip, cut 12 **strip E's** 2^1/$_2$" x 11".
- Cut 1 strip 13^1/$_2$" wide. From this strip, cut 1 **rectangle C** 13^1/$_2$" x 20".
- Cut 6 **middle border strips** 1^1/$_2$" wide.

From solid black fabric:

- Cut 1 strip 10^1/$_2$" wide. From this strip, cut 1 **rectangle D** 10^1/$_2$" x 26".
- Cut 1 strip 8" wide. From this strip, cut 12 **strip F's** 2" x 8".
- Cut 6 **inner border strips** 1" wide.

From fabric for binding:

- Cut 7 **binding strips** 2^1/$_4$" wide.

MAKING THE BLOCKS

*Follow **Piecing**, page 43, and **Pressing**, page 44, to make bed runner top. Use ^{1}/$_4$" seam allowances throughout.*

1. Sew 1 **strip A** to each long edge of 1 **rectangle B** to make **Strip Set A**. Press seam allowances toward the rectangle. Cut across Strip Set A at 1^1/$_2$" intervals to make 12 **Unit 1's**.

Strip Set A

Unit 1 (make 12)

1 ^{1}/$_2$"

2. Sew 1 **strip D** to each short edge of 1 **rectangle A** to make **Unit 2**. Make 6 Unit 2's. Sew 1 Unit 1 to each long edge of Unit 2 to make **Unit 3**. Make 6 Unit 3's.

Unit 2 (make 6)

Unit 3 (make 6)

3. Sew 1 **strip B** to each long edge of 1 **rectangle D** to make **Strip Set B**. Press seam allowances toward the rectangle. Cut across Strip Set B at 2" intervals to make 12 **Unit 4's**.

Strip Set B

Unit 4
(make 12)

2"

4. Sew 1 **strip F** to each short edge of 1 **Unit 3** to make **Unit 5**. Make 6 Unit 5's. Sew 1 Unit 4 to each long edge of Unit 5 to make **Unit 6**. Make 6 Unit 6's.

Unit 5 (make 6)   **Unit 6** (make 6)

5. Sew 1 **strip C** to each long edge of 1 **rectangle C** to make **Strip Set C**. Press seam allowances toward the rectangle. Cut across Strip Set C at 2$\frac{1}{2}$" intervals to make 7 **Unit 7's**.

Strip Set C

Unit 7
(make 7)

2$\frac{1}{2}$"

6. Sew 1 **strip E** to each short edge of 1 **Unit 6** to make **Unit 8**. Make 6 Unit 8's. Sew 1 Unit 7 to the *right side* of Unit 8 to make a **Block**. Make 6 Blocks.

Unit 8 (make 6)   **Block** (make 6)

   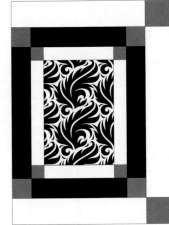

ASSEMBLING THE BED RUNNER TOP

Refer to Bed Runner Top Center Diagram to assemble bed runner top.

1. Sew 6 Blocks together. Sew the remaining Unit 7 to the left side to complete the **bed runner top center**.

2. Sew **inner border strips** together, end to end, to make 1 continuous strip.

3. To determine length of side inner borders, measure *length* across center of bed runner center. Cut 2 **side inner borders** from continuous strip. Matching centers and corners, sew side inner borders to bed runner center. Press seam allowances toward border.

4. To determine length of top/bottom inner border, measure *width* across center of bed runner center (including added borders). Cut 2 **top/bottom inner borders** from continuous strip. Matching centers and corners, sew top/bottom borders to bed runner center. Press seam allowances toward border.

5. In the same manner, use **middle border strips** to add side and then top/bottom middle borders to bed runner top. Press seam allowances toward border.

6. In the same manner, use **outer border strips** to add side and then top/bottom outer borders to bed runner top. Press seam allowances toward border.

COMPLETING THE QUILT

1. Follow **Quilting**, page 44, to mark, layer, and quilt as desired. Bed runner shown is quilted with an all-over feather pattern.

2. Use **binding strips** and follow **Making Straight Grain Binding**, page 46, to make binding. Follow **Attaching Binding with Mitered Corners**, page 46, to bind quilt.

Bed Runner Top Center

Top It Off Pillow Sham

Yardage amounts given and instructions are for making 2 pillow shams.

Finished Pillow Sham Size: 31" x 21" (79 cm x 53 cm)
Finished Block Size: 12½" x 17" (32 cm x 43 cm)

SHOPPING LIST

Yardage is based on 43"/44" (109 cm/112 cm) wide fabric with a usable width of 40" (102 cm).

- ☐ ³/₄ yd (69 cm) of black and white print fabric
- ☐ ¹/₄ yd (23 cm) of grey tone-on-tone fabric
- ☐ 1¹/₈ yds (1 m) of solid white fabric
- ☐ 1³/₄ yds (1.6 m) of solid black fabric
- ☐ Two 31¹/₂" x 21¹/₂" (80 cm x 55 cm) rectangles of fusible fleece

CUTTING THE PIECES

*Follow **Rotary Cutting**, page 42, to cut fabric. Cut all strips from the selvage-to-selvage width of the fabric. All measurements include ¹/₄" seam allowances.*

From black and white print fabric:
- Cut 1 strip 8¹/₂" wide. From this strip, cut 4 **rectangle A's** 6" x 8¹/₂".
- Cut 6 **border strips** 2¹/₂" wide.

From grey tone-on-tone print fabric:
- Cut 1 strip 1¹/₂" wide. From this strip, cut 2 **strip A's** 1¹/₂" x 15".
- Cut 1 strip 2" wide. From these strips, cut 2 **strip B's** 2" x 20".
- Cut 1 strip 2¹/₂" wide. From this strip, cut 2 **strip C's** 2¹/₂" x 16".

From solid white fabric:
- Cut 1 strip 8½" wide. From this strip, cut 1 **rectangle B** 8½" x 15". From remaining strip, cut 8 **strip D's** 1½" x 6".
- Cut 1 strip 11" wide. From this strip, cut 8 **strip E's** 2½" x 11".
- Cut 1 strip 13½" wide. From this strip, cut 1 **rectangle C** 13½" x 16".

From solid black fabric:
- Cut 4 **backing rectangles** 20" x 21½".
- Cut 1 strip 10½" wide. From this strip, cut 1 **rectangle D's** 10½" x 20" wide. From remainder of strip, cut 8 **strip F's** 2" x 8".

MAKING THE PILLOW SHAM TOP

Follow Piecing, page 43, and Pressing, page 44, to make pillow sham top. Use ¼" seam allowances throughout.

1. Repeat **Making the Blocks**, page 4, making 8 Unit 1's, 4 Unit 2's, 4 Unit 3's, 8 Unit 4's, 4 Unit 5's, 4 Unit 6's, and 6 Unit 7's to make 4 **Blocks**.

2. Sew 2 Blocks and 1 remaining Unit 7 together to complete the **pillow sham top center**.

Pillow Sham Top Center

3. Sew the **border strips** together, end to end, to make 1 continuous strip.

4. To determine length of side borders, measure *length* across center of pillow sham center. Cut 2 **side borders** from continuous strip. Matching centers and corners, sew side borders to pillow sham center. Press seam allowances toward border.

5. To determine length of top/bottom border, measure *width* across center of pillow sham center (including added borders). Cut 2 **top/bottom borders** from continuous strip. Matching centers and corners, sew top/bottom borders to pillow sham center. Press seam allowances toward border.

6. Repeat Steps 1-5 to make second pillow sham top.

COMPLETING THE PILLOW SHAM

1. Follow manufacturer's instructions to fuse fleece to pillow sham top.

2. Follow **Quilting**, page 44, to mark, layer, and quilt as desired. Pillow Sham shown is quilted with an all-over feather pattern.

3. On each backing rectangle, press 1 long edge ½" to wrong side; press ½" to wrong side again and stitch in place.

4. Matching right sides and overlapping hemmed edges, pin backing rectangles and sham top together. Sew around sham using a ¼" seam allowance. Clip corners and turn sham right side out; press.

5. Topstitch along edge of pillow sham; insert pillow.

Pillow Sham Top Diagram

Stepping Stones Bed Runner

Finished Bed Runner Size: 75" x 31" (191 cm x 79 cm)
Finished Block A Size: 6" x 22" (15 cm x 56 cm)
Finished Block B Size: 12" x 22" (30 cm x 56 cm)

SHOPPING LIST

Yardage is based on 43"/44" (109 cm/112 cm) wide fabric with a usable width of 40" (102 cm). Fat quarters are approximately 22" x 18" (56 cm x 46 cm).

- ☐ 4 assorted pink batik print fat quarters (includes binding)
- ☐ 1 green batik print fat quarter (includes binding)
- ☐ 1^{1}/$_{4}$ yds (1.1 m) of solid white fabric
- ☐ ^{3}/$_{4}$ yd (69 cm) of batik print fabric for outer border
- ☐ 2^{3}/$_{8}$ yds (2.2 m) of fabric for backing
- ☐ 83" x 39" (211 cm x 99 cm) piece of batting

CUTTING THE PIECES

*Follow **Rotary Cutting**, page 42, to cut fabric. For yardage, cut all strips from the selvage-to-selvage width of the fabric. For fat quarters, cut strips parallel to the short side. If using a directional print, pieces cut from fat quarters should be cut in the direction of the print. All measurements include ^{1}/$_{4}$" seam allowances.*

From fat quarter #1 (pink):
- Cut 1 **binding strip** 2^{1}/$_{4}$" x 18".
- Cut 8 **rectangle A's** 4^{1}/$_{2}$" x 8^{1}/$_{2}$".

From fat quarter #2 (pink):
- Cut 4 **binding strips** 2^{1}/$_{4}$" x 18".
- Cut 3 **rectangle A's** 4^{1}/$_{2}$" x 8^{1}/$_{2}$".

From fat quarter #3 (pink):
- Cut 1 **binding strip** 2^{1}/$_{4}$" x 18".
- Cut 3 **strip A's** 6^{1}/$_{2}$" x 18".

From fat quarter #4 (pink):
- Cut 1 **binding strip** 2^{1}/$_{4}$" x 18".
- Cut 3 **strip A's** 6^{1}/$_{2}$" x 18".

From fat quarter #5 (green):
- Cut 6 **binding strips** 2^{1}/$_{4}$" x 18".
- Cut 3 **strip B's** 2^{1}/$_{2}$" x 18".

From solid white fabric:
- Cut 5 strips 2^{1}/$_{2}$" wide. From this strip, cut 10 **strip A's** 2^{1}/$_{2}$" x 18".
- Cut 1 strip 8^{1}/$_{2}$" wide. From this strip, cut 22 **strip B's** 1^{1}/$_{2}$" x 8^{1}/$_{2}$".
- Cut 1 strip 6^{1}/$_{2}$" wide. From this strip, cut 22 **strip C's** 1^{1}/$_{2}$" x 6^{1}/$_{2}$".
- Cut 6 **inner border strips** 1^{1}/$_{2}$" wide.

From outer border fabric:
- Cut 6 **outer border strips** 3^{1}/$_{2}$" wide.

MAKING THE BLOCKS

*Follow **Piecing**, page 43, and **Pressing**, page 44, to make bed runner top. Use 1/4" seam allowances throughout.*

1. Sew 1 white **strip A** to each long edge of 1 fat quarter #5 **strip B** to make **Strip Set A**. Make 3 Strip Set A's. Cut across Strip Set A at 6½" intervals to make 6 **Unit 1**'s. Cut across remaining Strip Set A's at 2½" intervals to make 4 **Unit 2**'s.

Strip Set A (make 3)

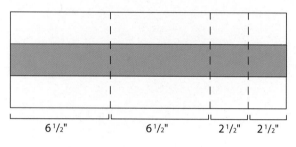

Unit 1 (make 6) **Unit 2** (make 4)

2. Sew 1 white **strip B** to each long edge of 1 fat quarter #1 **rectangle A** to make **Unit 3**. Make 8 **Unit 3**'s.

Unit 3 (make 8)

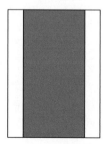

3. Sew 1 white **strip C** to top and bottom of Unit 3 to make **Unit 4**. Make 8 Unit 4's.

Unit 4 (make 8)

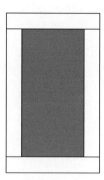

4. Repeat Steps 2-3 using fat quarter #2 **rectangle A** to make **Unit 5**. Make 3 Unit 5's.

Unit 5 (make 3)

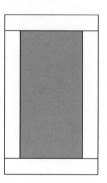

Sew 2 white **strip A's** and 3 fat quarter #3 **strip A's** together to make **Strip Set B**. Cut across Strip Set B at 3¹/₂" intervals to make 4 **Unit 6's**.

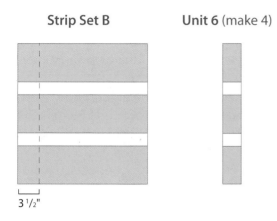

Strip Set B   Unit 6 (make 4)

3¹/₂"

Sew 2 white **strip A's** and 3 fat quarter #4 **strip A's** together make **Strip Set C**. Cut across Strip Set C at 3¹/₂" intervals to make 4 **Unit 7's**.

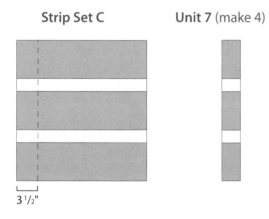

Strip Set C   Unit 7 (make 4)

3¹/₂"

7. Sew 2 **Unit 4's** and 1 **Unit 2** together make **Unit 8**. Make 4 **Unit 8's**.

Unit 8 (make 4)

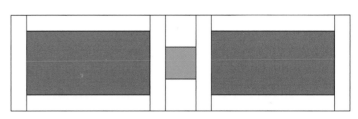

8. Sew 2 **Unit 1's** and 1 **Unit 5** together make **Block A**. Make 3 **Block A's**.

Block A (make 3)

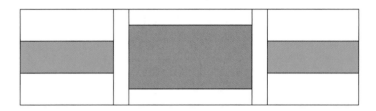

9. Sew 1 **Unit 6**, 1 **Unit 7**, and 1 **Unit 8** together make **Block B**. Make 4 **Block B's**.

Block B (make 4)

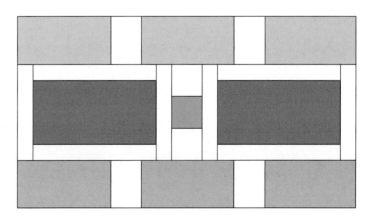

ASSEMBLING THE BED RUNNER TOP

*Refer to **Bed Runner Top Center Diagram** to assemble bed runner top center.*

1. Alternating blocks, sew Block A's and Block B's together to make **bed runner center.**

2. Sew **inner border strips** together, end to end, to make 1 continuous strip.

3. To determine length of side inner borders, measure *length* across center of bed runner top center. Cut 2 **side inner borders** from continuous strip. Matching centers and corners, sew side inner borders to bed runner top center. Press seam allowances toward border.

4. To determine length of top/bottom inner border, measure *width* across center of bed runner center (including added borders). Cut 2 **top/bottom inner borders** from continuous strip. Matching centers and corners, sew top/bottom borders to bed runner center. Press seam allowances toward border.

5. In the same manner, use **outer border strips** to add side and then top/bottom outer borders to bed runner top. Press seam allowances toward border.

COMPLETING THE BED RUNNER

1. Follow **Quilting**, page 44, to mark, layer, and quilt as desired. Bed runner shown is quilted with an all-over swirl pattern.

2. Use **binding strips** and follow **Making Straight Grain Binding**, page 46, to make binding. Follow **Attaching Binding with Mitered Corners**, page 46, to bind bed runner.

Bed Runner Top Center

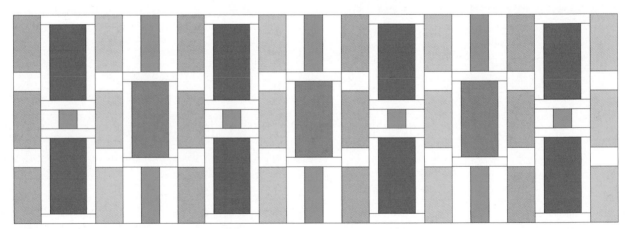

Stepping Stones Pillow Sham

Yardage amounts given and instructions are for making 2 pillow shams.

Finished Pillow Sham Size: 32" x 22" (81 cm x 56 cm)
Finished Block A Size: 6" x 20" (15 cm x 51 cm)
Finished Block B Size: 12" x 20" (30 cm x 51 cm)

SHOPPING LIST

Yardage is based on 43"/44" (109 cm/112 cm) wide fabric with a usable width of 40" (102 cm). Fat quarters are approximately 22" x 18" (56 cm x 46 cm).

- ☐ 4 assorted pink batik print fat quarters
- ☐ 1 green batik print fat quarters
- ☐ 4 yds (3.7 m) of solid white fabric
- ☐ Two 32¹/₂" x 22¹/₂" (83 cm x 57 cm) pieces of fusible fleece

CUTTING THE PIECES

*Follow **Rotary Cutting**, page 42, to cut fabric. For yardage, cut all strips from the selvage-to-selvage width of the fabric. For fat quarters, cut strips parallel to the 18" side. If using a directional print, pieces cut from fat quarters should be cut in the direction of the print. All measurements include ¹/₄" seam allowances.*

From fat quarter #1 (pink):
- Cut 8 **rectangle A's** 4¹/₂" x 7¹/₂".

From fat quarter #2 (pink):
- Cut 2 **rectangle A's** 4¹/₂" x 7¹/₂".

From fat quarter #3 (pink):
- Cut 3 **strip A's** 6¹/₂" x 21".

From fat quarter #4 (pink):
- Cut 3 **strip A's** 6¹/₂" x 21".

From fat quarter #5 (green batik print):
- Cut 2 **strip B's** 2¹/₂" x 21".

From solid white fabric:
- Cut 4 strips 2¹/₂" wide. From this strip, cut 4 **strip A's** 2¹/₂" x 21".
- Cut 1 strip 7¹/₂" wide. From this strip, cut 20 **strip B's** 1¹/₂" x 7¹/₂".
- Cut 1 strip 6¹/₂" wide. From these strips, cut 20 **strip C's** 1¹/₂" x 6¹/₂".
- Cut 4 strips 1¹/₂" wide. From these strips, cut 4 **strip D's** 1¹/₂" x 21".
- Cut 6 **border strips** 1¹/₂" wide.
- Cut 4 **backing rectangles** 22¹/₂" x 40".

MAKING THE PILLOW SHAM TOP

*Follow **Piecing**, page 43, and **Pressing**, page 44, to make pillow sham top. Use ¹/₄" seam allowances throughout.*

1. Repeat **Making the Blocks**, page 12, making 2 Strip Set A's, 4 Unit 1's, 4 Unit 2's, 8 Unit 3's, and 8 Unit 4's. Make 2 Unit 5's. Use fat quarter #3 strip A's and strip D's to make 1 Strip Set B and 4 Unit 6's. Use fat quarter #4 strip A's and strip D's to make 1 Strip Set C and 4 Unit 7's. Make 4 Unit 8's. With green strip placed horizontally, trim Unit 1's to 6" wide. Sew 2 Unit 1's and 1 Unit 5 together to make Block A. Sew 1 Unit 6, 1 Unit 7, and 1 Unit 8 together to make Block B. Make 4 Block B's.

2. Sew the Blocks together to complete the pillow sham top center. Make 2 pillow sham top centers.

Pillow Sham Top Center

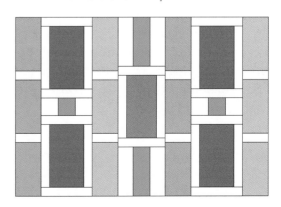

15

3. Sew the border strips together, end to end, to make 1 continuous strip.

4. To determine length of side borders, measure *length* across center of pillow sham center. Cut 2 **side borders** from continuous strip. Matching centers and corners, sew side borders to pillow sham center. Press seam allowances toward border.

5. To determine length of top/bottom border, measure *width* across center of pillow sham center (including added borders). Cut 2 **top/bottom borders** from continuous strip. Matching centers and corners, sew top/bottom borders to pillow sham center. Press seam allowances toward border.

COMPLETING THE PILLOW SHAM

1. Follow manufacturer's instructions to fuse fleece to wrong side of pillow sham top.

2. Follow **Quilting**, page 44, to mark, layer, and quilt as desired (optional). Pillow sham shown is quilted with topstitching 1/4" inside each colored area and evenly spaced lines in all white areas.

3. On each **backing rectangle**, press 1 long edge 1/2" to wrong side; press 1/2" to wrong side again and stitch i place.

4. Matching right sides and overlapping hemmed edge pin backing rectangles and sham top together. Sew around sham using a 1/4" seam allowance. Clip corner and turn sham right side out; press.

5. Topstitch along edge of pillow sham; insert pillow.

Dragon's Lair Bed Runner

Finished Bed Runner Size: 80" x 29" (203 cm x 74 cm)
Finished Block Size: 5" x 20" (13 cm x 51 cm)

SHOPPING LIST

Yardage is based on 43"/44" (109 cm/112 cm) wide fabric with a usable width of 40" (102 cm). Fat quarters are approxiimately 22" x 18" (56 cm x 46 cm).

☐ ¹/₄ yd (23 cm) *each* of 12 assorted print fabrics [or ⁵/₈ yd (57 cm) *each* if using directional fabric]

☐ 1¹/₈ yds (1 m) of fabric for background and sashing

☐ ³/₄ yd (69 cm) of fabric for outside border

☐ 2¹/₂ yds (2.3 m) of fabric for backing

☐ ¹/₂ yd (46 cm) of fabric for binding

☐ 88" x 37" (224 cm x 94 cm) piece of batting

CUTTING THE PIECES

*Follow **Rotary Cutting**, page 42, to cut fabric. Cut all strips from the selvage-to-selvage width of the fabric. If using a directional print, pieces cut from fat quarters should be cut in the direction of the print. All measurements include ¹/₄" seam allowances.*

From each assorted print fabric:
* Cut 1 **rectangle** 5¹/₂" x 20¹/₂".

From background and sashing fabric:
* Cut 1 strip 20¹/₂" wide. From this strip, cut 13 **vertical sashings** 1¹/₂" x 20¹/₂".
* Cut 4 **horizontal sashings** 1¹/₂" wide.
* Cut 3 strips 2¹/₂" wide. From these strips, cut 48 **block corners** 2¹/₂" x 2¹/₂".

From border fabric:
* Cut 6 **outer border strips** 3¹/₂" wide.

From binding fabric:
* Cut 6 **binding strips** 2¹/₂" wide.

MAKING THE BLOCKS

*Follow **Piecing**, page 43, and **Pressing**, page 44, to make bed runner top. Use ¹/₄" seam allowances throughout.*

1. Draw a diagonal line on the wrong side of each **block corner**.

2. Pin 1 block corner on each corner of one **rectangle**; sew along drawn line (**Fig. 1**). Trim excess fabric ¹/₄" from seamline (**Fig. 2**); press open. Repeat for each corner to make a **Block**. Make 12 blocks.

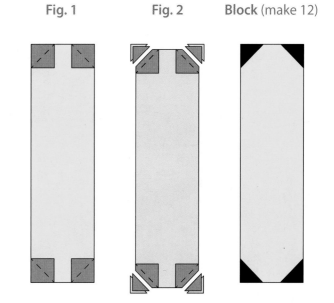

Fig. 1   Fig. 2   Block (make 12)

ADDING THE BORDERS

1. Sew 12 blocks and 13 **vertical sashings** together.

2. Sew 4 **horizontal sashings** together end to end. To determine length of top and bottom sashings, measure width across center of bed runner. From continuous horizontal sashings, cut 2 top/bottom sashings the determined length.

3. Matching centers and corners, sew top and bottom sashings to bed runner.

4. Sew 6 **outer border strips** together end to end. To determine length of side outer borders, measure from top to bottom across center of bed runner. From continuous outer border strip, cut 2 side outer borders the determined length.

5. Sew side outer borders to bed runner.

6. To determine length of top/bottom outer borders, measure from side to side across center of bed runner. From continuous outer border strip, cut 2 top/bottom outer borders the determined length.

7. Sew top and bottom outer borders to bed runner.

COMPLETING THE BED RUNNER

1. Follow **Quilting**, page 44, to mark, layer, and quilt as desired. Our Bed Runner is quilted with an all-over circular pattern.

2. Use **binding strips** and follow **Making Straight Grain Binding**, page 46, to make binding. Follow **Attaching Binding with Mitered Corners**, page 46, to bind quilt.

Bed Runner Top

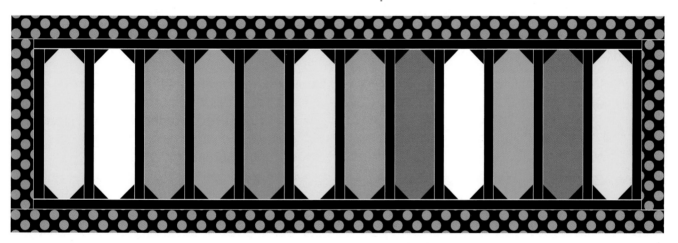

Variable Star Table Runner

This pattern was designed to use Moda Turnovers®. A Turnover is a package of forty 6" (15 cm) squares cut in half diagonally. You can easily cut your own triangles from fat quarters or your scrap basket. Also, Moda Charm Squares® work great for the 5" squares.

Finished Table Runner Size: 15$\frac{1}{2}$" x 44$\frac{1}{2}$" (39 cm x 113 cm)
Finished Block Size: 13$\frac{1}{2}$" x 13$\frac{1}{2}$" (34 cm x 34 cm)

SHOPPING LIST

Yardage is based on 43"/44" (109 cm/112 cm) wide fabric with a usable width of 40" (102 cm).

☐ *12 assorted print triangles **or** 6 or more assorted 6" x 6" (15 cm x 15 cm) print squares cut in half diagonally

☐ Three 5" x 5" (13 cm x 13 cm) squares of print fabric

☐ $\frac{1}{2}$ yd (46 cm) of ecru fabric for background

☐ $\frac{1}{2}$ yd (46 cm) of print fabric for sashings, borders, and binding

☐ 23$\frac{1}{2}$" x 52$\frac{1}{2}$" (60 cm x 133 cm) piece of fabric for backing

☐ 23$\frac{1}{2}$" x 52$\frac{1}{2}$" (60 cm x 133 cm) piece of batting

* If using squares, more squares will provide more variety.

CUTTING THE PIECES

*Follow **Rotary Cutting**, page 42, to cut fabric. Cut all strips from the selvage-to-selvage width of the fabric. Borders are cut exact length. All measurements include $\frac{1}{4}$" seam allowances.*

From ecru fabric:
- Cut 6 squares 6" x 6". Cut each square in half diagonally to make 12 **triangles**.
- Cut 2 strips 5" wide. From these strips, cut 12 **squares** 5" x 5".

From sashing, border, and binding fabric:
- Cut 2 **sashings** 1$\frac{1}{2}$" x 14".
- Cut 2 **top/bottom borders** 1$\frac{1}{2}$" x 43", pieced as needed.
- Cut 2 **side borders** 1$\frac{1}{2}$" x 16".
- Cut 4 **binding strips** 2$\frac{1}{4}$" wide.

MAKING THE BLOCKS

*Follow **Piecing**, page 43, and **Pressing**, page 44, to make table runner top. Use ¹/₄" seam allowances throughout.*

1. Sew 1 print **triangle** and 1 ecru **triangle** together to make 1 **Triangle-Square**. Make 12 Triangle-Squares.

Triangle-Square (make 12)

2. Refer to **Fig. 1** to cut each Triangle-Square in half diagonally to make 24 **triangles**.

Fig. 1

3. Sew 2 assorted **triangles** together to make a **Four-Triangle Unit**. Make 12 Four-Triangle Units. Trim each Four-Triangle Unit to 5" x 5".

Four-Triangle Unit (make 12)

4. Sew 2 ecru **squares** and 1 Four-Triangle Unit together to make **Row A**. Make 6 assorted Row A's.

Row A (make 6)

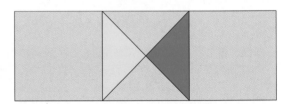

5. Sew 2 Four-Triangle Units and 1 print square together to make **Row B**. Make 3 assorted Row B's.

Row B (make 3)

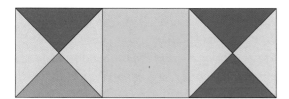

6. Sew 2 Row A's and 1 Row B together to make a **Block**. Make 3 Blocks.

Block (make 3)

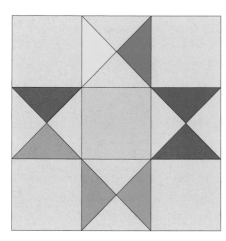

ASSEMBLING THE TABLE RUNNER TOP

1. Sew 3 Blocks and 2 **sashings** together to make table runner top center.

Table Runner Top Center

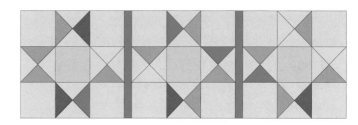

2. Sew **top** and **bottom borders** to table runner top center.

3. Sew **side borders** to table runner top center.

COMPLETING THE TABLE RUNNER

1. Follow **Quilting**, page 44, to mark, layer, and quilt as desired. Table Runner shown is quilted along each edge of the border and with an all-over meandering pattern in the table runner top center.

2. Use **binding strips** and follow **Making Straight Grain Binding**, page 46, to make binding. Follow **Attaching Binding with Mitered Corners**, page 46, to bind quilt.

Eight-Point Star Wallhanging

This pattern was designed to use Moda Turnovers®. A Turnover is a package of forty 6" squares cut in half diagonally. You can easily cut your own triangles from fat quarters or your scrap basket.

Finished Wallhanging Size: 30" x 30" (76 cm x 76 cm) excluding points
Finished Eight Point Star Block Size: 20" x 20" (51 cm x 51 cm)

SHOPPING LIST

Yardage is based on 43"/44" (109 cm/112 cm) wide fabric with a usable width of 40" (102 cm).

☐ *56 assorted print triangles **or** 28 or more assorted 6" x 6" (15 cm x 15 cm) print squares cut in half diagonally

☐ ³/₈ yd (34 cm) of ecru fabric for background

☐ 1¹/₈ yds (1 m) of fabric for backing

☐ ³/₈ yd (34 cm) of print fabric for binding

☐ 38" x 38" (97 cm x 97 cm) piece of batting

* If using squares, more squares will provide more variety.

CUTTING THE PIECES

*Follow **Rotary Cutting**, page 42, to cut fabric. Cut all strips from the selvage-to-selvage width of the fabric. All measurements include ¹/₄" seam allowances.*

From ecru fabric:
- Cut 4 squares 6" x 6". Cut each square in half diagonally to make 8 **triangles**.
- Cut 4 **squares** 5¹/₂" x 5¹/₂".

From fabric for backing:
- Cut **backing** 38" x 38".

From binding fabric:
- Cut 4 **binding strips** 2¹/₄" wide.

MAKING THE BLOCKS

*Follow **Piecing**, page 43, and **Pressing**, page 44, to make wallhanging top. Fabric placement is important for the Wallhanging Center. You may prefer to lay out your triangles to determine placement before sewing your Triangle-Squares. Use ¹/₄" seam allowances throughout.*

1. Sew 2 print **triangles** together to make 1 **Triangle-Square A**. Make 24 Triangle-Square A's. Trim Triangle-Square A's to 5¹/₂" x 5¹/₂".

Triangle-Square A (make 24)

2. Sew 1 print **triangle** and 1 ecru **triangle** together to make 1 **Triangle-Square B**. Make 8 Triangle-Square B's. Trim Triangle-Square B's to 5¹/₂" x 5¹/₂".

Triangle-Square B (make 8)

3. Sew 2 **squares** and 2 Triangle Square B's together to make **Row A**.

Row A

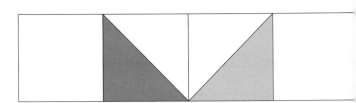

4. Sew 2 **Triangle-Square A's** and 2 **Triangle Square B's** together to make Row B.

Row B

5. Sew 2 **Triangle-Square A's** and 2 **Triangle Square B's** together to make Row C.

Row C

6. Sew 2 **squares** and 2 Triangle Square B's together to make Row D.

Row D

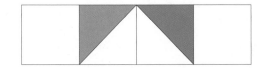

7. Sew **Rows** together to make the wallhanging center.

Wallhanging Center

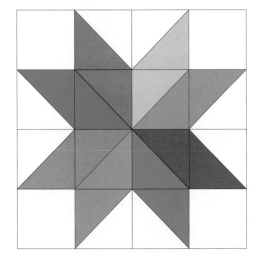

ADDING THE BORDERS

1. Sew 4 Triangle-Square A's together make top border. Repeat to make bottom border.

Top/Bottom Border (make 2)

2. Sew 6 Triangle-Square A's together make a side border. Repeat to make another Side Border.

Side Border (make 2)

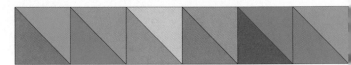

3. Sew top and bottom border to wallhanging center. Sew 1 side border to each side of wallhanging center.

COMPLETING THE WALLHANGING

1. Follow **Quilting**, page 44, to mark, layer, and quilt as desired. Wallhanging shown is quilted with an all-over meandering pattern.

2. Follow **Making a Hanging Sleeve**, page 46, to make and attach a hanging sleeve, if desired.

3. Use **binding strips** and follow **Making Straight Grain Binding**, page 46, to make binding. Follow **Attaching Binding with Mitered Corners**, page 46, to bind wallhanging.

Pinwheels Table Runner

This pattern was designed to use Moda Turnovers®. A Turnover is a package of forty 6" squares cut in half diagonally. You can easily cut your own triangles from fat quarters or your scrap basket. Also, Moda Charm Squares® work great for the 5" squares.

Finished Table Runner Size: 12" x 32" (30 cm x 81 cm) excluding Prairie Points
Finished Block Size: 10" x 10" (25 cm x 25 cm)

SHOPPING LIST

Yardage is based on 43"/44" (109 cm/112 cm) wide fabric with a usable width of 40" (102 cm).

- ☐ *12 assorted print triangles **or** 6 or more assorted 6" x 6" (15 cm x 15 cm) print squares cut in half diagonally
- ☐ 24 assorted 5" x 5" (13 cm x 13 cm) print squares for Prairie Points
- ☐ ¹/₄ yd (23 cm) of ecru fabric for background
- ☐ ¹/₄ yd (23 cm) of print fabric for outer border
- ☐ 12¹/₂" x 32¹/₂" (32 cm x 83 cm) piece of fabric for backing
- ☐ 12¹/₂" x 32¹/₂" (32 cm x 83 cm) piece of batting
- ☐ Three 2" (51 mm) diameter buttons
* If using squares, more squares will provide more variety.

CUTTING THE PIECES

*Follow **Rotary Cutting**, page 42, to cut fabric. Cut all strips from the selvage-to-selvage width of the fabric. All measurements include ¹/₄" seam allowances.*

From ecru fabric:
- Cut 6 squares 6" x 6". Cut each square in half diagonally to make 12 **triangles.**

From outer border fabric:
- Cut 2 **side borders** 1¹/₂" x 12¹/₂".
- Cut 2 **top/bottom borders** 1¹/₂" x 30¹/₂".

MAKING THE BLOCKS

*Follow **Piecing**, page 43, and **Pressing**, page 44, to make table runner top. Use ¹/₄" seam allowances throughout.*

1. Sew 1 print **triangle** and 1 ecru **triangle** together to make 1 Triangle-Square. Make 12 Triangle-Squares.

Triangle-Square (make 12)

2. Sew 4 Triangle-Squares together to make a Block. Make 3 Blocks. Trim each Block to 10¹/₂" x 10¹/₂".

Block (make 3)

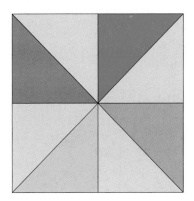

3. Sew **Blocks** together to make the **Table Runner Top Center**.

Table Runner Top Center

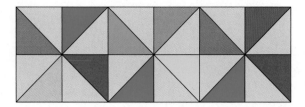

4. Sew **top** and **bottom borders** to table runner top center.

5. Sew **side borders** to table runner top center.

ADDING THE PRAIRIE POINTS

1. Matching wrong sides, fold a 5" square from corner to corner (**Fig. 1**).

Fig. 1

2. Fold from corner to corner again (**Fig. 2**). Make 24 Prairie Points.

Fig. 2

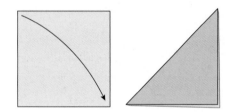

3. Spacing points evenly and tucking Prairie Points inside previous point where possible, pin 9 Prairie Points *each* to top and bottom and 3 Prairie Points *each* to sides of Table Runner Top (**Fig. 3**).

Fig. 3

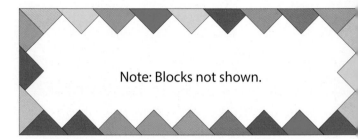

Note: Blocks not shown.

4. Baste Prairie Points in place ¹/₄" from edges of table runner.

COMPLETING THE TABLE RUNNER

1. Matching right sides, place table runner top and backing together with Prairie Points layered inside. Place layers on batting. Pin layers together.

2. Sew around all sides of top, leaving an 8" opening on one long side for turning. Turn right side out and sew opening closed; press.

3. Follow **Quilting**, page 44, to mark and quilt as desired. Table Runner shown is quilted along each edge of the border and with an all-over meandering pattern in the table runner top center.

4. Sew buttons to center of each pinwheel.

Classic Table Runner

Finished Table Runner Size: 36" x 15¹/₂" (91 cm x 39 cm)
Finished Block Size: 12¹/₂" x 12¹/₂" (32 cm x 32 cm)

CUTTING THE PIECES

*Follow **Rotary Cutting**, page 42, to cut fabric. Cut all strips from the selvage-to-selvage width of the fabric. All measurements include ¹/₄" seam allowances.*

From dark fabric:
- Cut 4 **long strips** 1¹/₂" wide.
- Cut 1 strip 3" wide. From this strip, cut 8 **squares** 3" x 3".
- Cut 1 strip 6¹/₂" wide. From this strip, cut 1 **large rectangle** 6¹/₂" x 13". From remaining width, cut 2 **side borders** 2¹/₂" x 13".
- Cut 2 strips 1¹/₂ wide. From these strips, cut 2 **top/bottom borders** 1¹/₂" x 35¹/₂".
- Cut 4 **binding strips** 2¹/₂" wide.

From light fabric:
- Cut 4 **long strips** 1¹/₂" wide.
- Cut 2 strips 3" wide. From these strips, cut 18 **squares** 3" x 3".

MAKING THE BLOCKS

*Use the Strip Tube Junior™ ruler **or** follow **Template Cutting**, page 43, to cut a plastic template from the pattern below. Follow **Piecing**, page 43, and **Pressing**, page 44, to make table runner top. Use ¹/₄" seam allowances throughout.*

1. Sew 1 light **long strip** and 1 dark **long strip** together to make a **Strip Set**. Make 4 Strip Sets.

Strip Set (make 4)

2. Matching right sides and alternating colors, sew 2 Strip Sets together along each long edge (**Figs 1-2**). Make 2 sets.

Fig. 1   Fig. 2

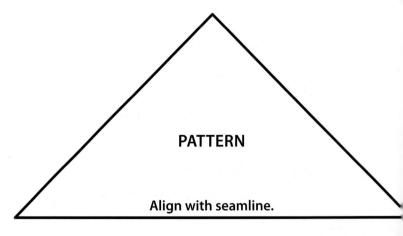

PATTERN

Align with seamline.

3. Place Strip Tube ruler **or** template along seamline (Fig. 3). If using the Strip Tube Ruler, align the 3" mark on the ruler with the seamline. If using the template, align the long side of the template with the seamline. Cut along the diagonal sides of the template or ruler (Fig. 4).

Fig. 3

Fig. 4

4. Rotate the template or ruler and slide it over a bit. Cut along the diagonal sides of the template or ruler (Fig. 5). Cut 12 in each position for a total of 24.

Fig. 5

5. Press each square open to make 12 **Unit 1's** and 12 **Unit 2's**.

Unit 1 (make 12)

Unit 2 (make 12)

6. Sew 3 light **squares** and 2 Unit 1's together to make **Row A**. Make 6 Row A's. Press seam allowances toward the light square.

Row A (make 6)

7. Sew 2 dark **squares** and 3 Unit 2's together to make **Row B**. Make 4 Row B's. Press seam allowances toward the dark square.

Row B (make 4)

3. Sew Row A's and Row B's together to make a Block. Make 2 Blocks.

Block (make 2)

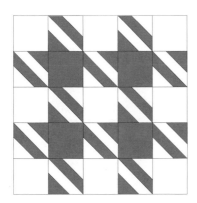

ASSEMBLING THE TABLE RUNNER TOP

Refer to Table Runner Top Diagram to assemble table runner top.

1. Sew 2 Blocks and the **large rectangle** together to make **Unit 3**. Press seam allowances towards the large rectangle.

Unit 3

2. Sew a **side border** on each side of Unit 3. Press seam allowances toward the side borders.

3. Matching centers and corners, sew **top/bottom borders** to table runner center. Press seam allowances toward border.

COMPLETING THE QUILT

1. Follow **Quilting**, page 44, to mark, layer, and quilt as desired. Table runner shown is quilted in the ditch around each square. The large rectangle between the blocks is quilted in a grid of approximately 1" squares and there is a straight line quilted in each side border.

2. Use **binding strips** and follow **Making Straight Grain Binding**, page 46, to make binding. Follow **Attaching Binding with Mitered Corners**, page 46, to bind quilt.

Table Runner Top

Classic Placemats

Yardage amounts given and instructions are for making 2 placemats.

Finished Placemat Size: $18^1/2$" x $13^1/2$" (47 cm x 34 cm)
Finished Block Size: $12^1/2$" x $12^1/2$" (32 cm x 32 cm)

SHOPPING LIST

Yardage is based on 43"/44" (109 cm/112 cm) wide fabric with a usable width of 40" (102 cm).

- ☐ $^3/4$ yd (69 cm) of dark fabric (includes binding)
- ☐ $^3/8$ yd (34 cm) of light fabric
- ☐ $^3/4$ yd (69 cm) of fabric for backing
- ☐ Two 23" x 18" (58 cm x 46 cm) pieces of batting
- ☐ Strip Tube Junior™ ruler (CozyQuilt.com) **or** template plastic and a permanent pen

CUTTING THE PIECES

*Follow **Rotary Cutting**, page 42, to cut fabric. Cut all strips from the selvage-to-selvage width of the fabric. All measurements include $^1/4$" seam allowances.*

From dark fabric:
- Cut 4 **long strips** $1^1/2$" wide.
- Cut 1 strip 3" wide. From this strip, cut 8 **squares** 3" x 3".
- Cut 1 strip $5^1/2$" wide. From this strip, cut 2 **rectangles** $5^1/2$" x 13".
- Cut 4 **binding strips** $2^1/2$" wide.

From light fabric:
- Cut 4 **long strips** $1^1/2$" wide.
- Cut 2 strips 3" wide. From these strips, cut 18 **squares** 3" x 3".

From backing fabric:
- Cut 2 **backings** 23" x 18".

MAKING THE PLACEMAT

*Follow **Piecing**, page 43, and **Pressing**, page 44, to make placemat top. Use $1/4$" seam allowances throughout.*

1. Follow **Classic Table Runner**, Making the Blocks, page 30, to make 2 **Blocks**.

2. Sew 1 **rectangle** to one side of each Block to make placemat top.

Placemat Top

COMPLETING THE QUILT

1. Follow **Quilting**, page 44, to mark, layer, and quilt as desired. Placemats shown are quilted in the ditch around each square and the rectangle is quilted in a grid of approximately 1" squares.

2. Use **binding strips** and follow **Making Straight Grain Binding**, page 46, to make binding. Follow **Attaching Binding with Mitered Corners**, page 46, to bind quilt

Picnic at the Farmer's Market Wallhanging

Finished Wallhanging Size: 39" x 39" (99 cm x 99 cm)
Finished Block Size: 8" x 8" (20 cm x 20 cm)

SHOPPING LIST

Yardage is based on 43"/44" (109 cm/112 cm) wide fabric with a usable width of 40" (102 cm).

☐ ¹/₄ yd (23 cm) **each** of 13 assorted print fabrics
☐ 2 yds (1.8 m) of solid black fabric
☐ 2⁵/₈ yds (2.4 m) of fabric for backing
☐ ³/₈ yd (34 cm) of fabric for binding
☐ 47" x 47" (119 cm x 119 cm) piece of batting

CUTTING THE PIECES

*Follow **Rotary Cutting**, page 42, to cut fabric. Cut all strips from the selvage-to-selvage width of the fabric. All measurements include ¹/₄" seam allowances.*

From *each* assorted print fabric:

- Cut 1 **center square** 4¹/₂" x 4¹/₂".
- Cut 1 strip 2¹/₂" wide. From this strip, cut 8 **squares** 2¹/₂" x 2¹/₂".

From solid black fabric:

- Cut 7 strips 2¹/₂" wide. From these strips, cut 52 **rectangles** 2¹/₂" x 4¹/₂".
- Cut 4 strips 2¹/₂" wide. From these strips, cut 52 **squares** 2¹/₂" x 2¹/₂".
- Cut 5 strips 1¹/₂" wide. From these strips, cut 18 **very short sashing strips** 1¹/₂" x 8¹/₂".
- Cut 1 strip 1¹/₂" wide. From this strip, cut 2 **short sashing strips** 1¹/₂" x 14".
- Cut 2 **medium sashing strips** 1¹/₂" x 32".
- Cut 2 **long sashing strips** 1¹/₂" x 50", piecing as needed.
- Cut 1 strip 13¹/₂" wide. From this strip, cut 2 squares 13¹/₂" x 13¹/₂". Cut each square *twice* diagonally to make 8 **side setting triangles**.
- Cut 1 strip 8" wide. From this strip, cut 2 squares 8" x 8". Cut each square *once* diagonally to make 2 **corner setting triangles**.

From fabric for binding:

- Cut 5 **binding strips** 2¹/₄" wide.

MAKING THE BLOCKS

*Follow **Piecing**, page 43, and **Pressing**, page 44, to make wallhanging top. Use ¹/₄" seam allowances throughout.*

1. Draw a diagonal line on the wrong side of each print fabric **square**. Place 1 marked square on the right corner of 1 **rectangle**. Sew on drawn line; trim ¹/₄" from stitching line (**Fig. 1**). Press open to make **Unit 1**. Make 4 matching Unit 1's.

Fig. 1

Unit 1 (make 4)

2. Place a matching print square on the left corner of 1 Unit 1 (**Fig. 2**). Sew on drawn line; trim ¹/₄" from stitching line. Press open to make Unit 2. Make 4 matching Unit 2's.

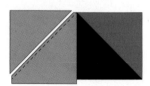

Fig. 2

Unit 2 (make 4 matching)

3. Sew 1 black **square** to each end of Unit 2 to make **Unit 3**. Make 2 Unit 3's.

Unit 3 (make 2)

4. Sew 1 Unit 2 to opposite sides of matching **center square** to make **Unit 4**.

5. Sew 1 Unit 3 to top and bottom of Unit 4 to make Block.

Unit 4

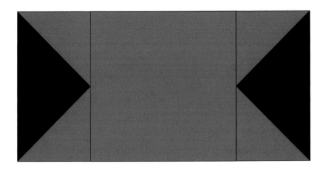

Block

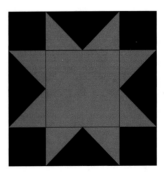

6. Repeat Steps 1-5 with each remaining print fabric to make a total of 13 Blocks.

ASSEMBLING THE WALLHANGING TOP

*Refer to **Wallhanging Top Diagram** to assemble wallhanging top.*

1. Sew Blocks, **very short sashings**, **side setting triangles**, and **corner setting triangles** together into *diagonal* Rows.

2. Sew Rows, remaining **sashings**, and corner setting triangles together to make **Wallhanging Top**. Square top to $38^{1}/_{2}$" x $38^{1}/_{2}$".

COMPLETING THE WALLHANGING

1. Follow **Quilting**, page 44, to mark, layer, and quilt as desired. Wallhanging shown is quilted with an all-over meandering pattern.

2. Follow **Making a Hanging Sleeve**, page 46, to make and attach a hanging sleeve, if desired.

3. Use **binding strips** and follow **Making Straight Grain Binding**, page 46, to make binding. Follow **Attaching Binding with Mitered Corners**, page 46, to bind quilt.

Wallhanging Top

Picnic at the Farmer's Market Placemats

Yardage amounts given and instructions are for making 4 placemats.

Finished Placemat Size: 18" x 14" (46 cm x 36 cm)
Finished Block Size: 4" x 4" (10 cm x 10 cm)

SHOPPING LIST

Yardage is based on 43"/44" (109 cm/112 cm) wide fabric with a usable width of 40" (102 cm).

☐ 1 yd (91 cm) **each** of 4 assorted print fabrics (includes binding)

☐ $^{3}/_{4}$ yd (69 cm) of solid black fabric
☐ Four 25" x 21" (64 cm x 53 cm) pieces of batting

CUTTING THE PIECES

*Follow **Rotary Cutting**, page 42, to cut fabric. Cut all strips from the selvage-to-selvage width of the fabric. All measurements include $^{1}/_{4}$" seam allowances.*

From *each* print fabric:
- Cut 2 **binding strips** $2^{1}/_{2}$" x 40".
- Cut 2 strips $1^{1}/_{2}$" wide. From these strips, cut 32 **squares** $1^{1}/_{2}$" x $1^{1}/_{2}$".
- Cut 1 **backing** 25" x 21".
- Cut 1 **large rectangle** $13^{1}/_{2}$" x $9^{1}/_{2}$".
- Cut 4 **center squares** $2^{1}/_{2}$" x $2^{1}/_{2}$".
- Cut 1 **pocket lining** $4^{1}/_{2}$" x $6^{1}/_{2}$".
- Cut 1 **pocket binding** 1" x $4^{1}/_{2}$".
- Cut 1 **pocket accent** $2^{1}/_{2}$" x $4^{1}/_{2}$".

From solid black fabric:
- Cut 3 strips $1^{1}/_{2}$" wide. From these strips, cut 64 **squares** $1^{1}/_{2}$" x $1^{1}/_{2}$".
- Cut 4 strips $1^{1}/_{2}$" wide. From these strips, cut 64 **rectangles** $1^{1}/_{2}$" x $2^{1}/_{2}$".
- Cut 1 strip 1" wide. From these strips, cut 8 **sashings** 1" x $4^{1}/_{2}$".
- Cut 2 strips $4^{1}/_{2}$" wide. From these strips, cut 4 **placemat accents** $4^{1}/_{2}$" x $13^{1}/_{2}$".

MAKING THE PLACEMAT TOP

*Follow **Piecing**, page 43, and **Pressing**, page 44, to make placemat top. Use ¹⁄₄" seam allowances throughout.*

1. Follow **Making the Blocks**, page 36, using print **squares** and **center squares**, and black **squares** and **rectangles** to make 4 **Blocks**.

2. Sew 3 Blocks and 2 **sashings** together to make Unit 1.

Unit 1

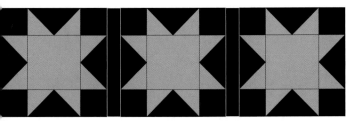

3. Sew 1 **pocket accent** to the remaining Block to make Unit 2.

Unit 2

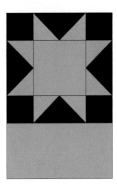

4. Matching wrong sides, layer Unit 2 and **pocket lining**; baste along upper edge.

5. Press 1 long edge of **pocket binding** ¹⁄₄" to wrong side.

6. Sew long raw edge of pocket binding to basted edge of Unit 2/pocket lining. Fold binding to wrong side of pocket; hand stitch in place.

7. Matching bottom edges, layer wrong side of pocket on right side of **placemat accent** to make Unit 3; baste along left side.

Unit 3

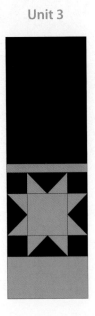

8. Sew Unit 1 to the **large rectangle** to make **Unit 4**.

Unit 4

9. Sew Unit 3 to Unit 4 to make **placemat top**.

Placemat Top

COMPLETING THE PLACEMAT

1. Follow **Quilting**, page 44, to mark, layer, and quilt as desired, folding pocket out of the way so that it is not caught in the quilting. Placemat shown is quilted with an all-over meandering pattern. Fold pocket into place and baste along side and bottom edges.

2. Use **binding strips** and follow **Making Straight Grain Binding**, page 46, to make binding. Follow **Attaching Binding with Mitered Corners**, page 46, to bind quilt.

NAPKINS

For each napkin, cut an 18" x 18" square of fabric. Press each edge 1/4" to wrong side; press 1/4" to wrong side again. Stitch around all sides.

Hot Pad

Finished Hot Pad Size: 8" x 8" (20 cm x 20 cm)

SHOPPING LIST

Yardage is based on 43"/44" (109 cm/112 cm) wide fabric with a usable width of 40" (102 cm).

- ☐ ¹/₄ yd (23 cm) of print fabric
- ☐ ¹/₄ yd (23 cm) of solid black fabric (includes binding)
- ☐ 9" x 9" (23 cm x 23 cm) piece of fabric for backing
- ☐ Two 9" x 9" (23 cm x 23 cm) pieces of batting

CUTTING THE PIECES

*Follow **Rotary Cutting**, page 42, to cut fabric. Cut all strips from the selvage-to-selvage width of the fabric. All measurements include ¹/₄" seam allowances.*

From print fabric:

- Cut 1 **center square** 4¹/₂" x 4¹/₂".
- Cut 1 strip 2¹/₂" wide. From this strip, cut 8 **squares** 2¹/₂" x 2¹/₂".

From solid black fabric:

- Cut 1 strip 2¹/₂" wide. From this strip, cut 4 **squares** 2¹/₂" x 2¹/₂" and 4 **rectangles** 2¹/₂" x 4¹/₂".
- Cut 1 **binding strip** 2¹/₄" wide.
- Cut 1 **hanging loop** 1" x 3".

MAKING THE BLOCK

*Follow **Piecing**, page 43, and **Pressing**, page 44, to make hot pad top. Use ¹/₄" seam allowances throughout.*

1. Follow **Making the Blocks**, page 36, using print **squares** and **center square and** black **squares** and **rectangles** to make a **Block**.

COMPLETING THE HOT PAD

1. Follow **Quilting**, page 44, to mark, layer, and quilt as desired. Hot Pad shown is quilted in the ditch around the star. Trim backing even with Block.

2. Use **binding strips** and follow **Making Straight Grain Binding**, page 46, to make binding. Follow **Attaching Binding with Mitered Corners**, page 46, to bind quilt.

3. Press each edge of **hanging loop** ¹/₄" to wrong side. Matching long edges, press loop in half so raw edges are inside. Stitch along folded edges. Matching short ends, fold loop in half; hand stitch ends to corner of hot pad.

General Instructions

To make your quilting easier and more enjoyable, we encourage you to carefully read all of the general instructions, study the color photographs, and familiarize yourself with the individual project instructions before beginning a project.

FABRICS

SELECTING FABRICS

Choose high-quality, medium-weight 100% cotton fabrics. All-cotton fabrics hold a crease better, fray less, and are easier to quilt than cotton/polyester blends.

Yardage requirements listed for each project are based on 43"/44" wide fabric with a "usable" width of 40" after shrinkage and trimming selvages. Actual usable width will probably vary slightly from fabric to fabric. Our recommended yardage lengths should be adequate for occasional re-squaring of fabric when many cuts are required.

PREPARING FABRICS

Pre-washing fabrics may cause edges to ravel. As a result, your precut fabrics may not be large enough to cut all of the pieces required for your chosen project. Therefore, we do not recommend pre-washing yardage or precut fabrics.

Before cutting, prepare fabrics with a steam iron set on cotton and starch or sizing. The starch or sizing will give the fabric a crisp finish. This will make cutting more accurate and may make piecing easier.

ROTARY CUTTING
CUTTING FROM YARDAGE

- Place fabric on work surface with fold closest to you.

- Cut all strips from the selvage-to-selvage width of the fabric unless otherwise indicated in project instructions.

- Square left edge of fabric using rotary cutter and rulers *(Figs. 1-2)*.

Fig. 1   Fig. 2

- To cut each strip required for a project, place ruler over cut edge of fabric, aligning desired marking on ruler with cut edge; make cut *(Fig. 3)*.

Fig. 3

- When cutting several strips from a single piece of fabric it is important to make sure that cuts remain at a perfect right angle to the fold; square fabric as needed.

CUTTING FROM PRECUTS

Many precut fabrics have pinked edges and most manufacturers include the points of the pinked edges in the measurement given on the label. Before cutting precuts into smaller pieces, measure your precuts to determine if you need to include the points to achieve the correct cut size.

If cutting strips parallel to the long edge, place fat quarter on work surface with short edge closest to you. Cut all strips parallel to the long edge of the fabric in the same manner as cutting from yardage unless otherwise indicated in project instructions.

To cut each strip, place ruler over cut edge of fabric, aligning desired marking on ruler with cut edge; make cut.

TEMPLATE CUTTING

Our template pattern has a solid cutting line.

1. To make a template from a pattern, use a permanent fine-point pen and a ruler to carefully trace pattern onto template plastic. Cut out template along inner edge of drawn line. Check template against original pattern for accuracy.
2. Place template on fabric. Cut out fabric piece using rotary cutting equipment.

PIECING

Precise cutting, followed by accurate piecing, will ensure that all the pieces of the quilt top fit together well.

Set sewing machine stitch length for approximately 11 stitches per inch.

Use neutral-colored general-purpose sewing thread (not quilting thread) in needle and in bobbin.

An accurate ¼" seam allowance is *essential*. Presser feet that are ¼" wide are available for most sewing machines.

For an accurate seam allowance when piecing precuts with pinked edges, measure from point to point across the center of the piece. If it measures the exact size, align the tip of the points with your ¼" seam guide when sewing. It may be necessary to use a "scant" ¼" seam allowance. Making a "test block" will determine if any adjustments to your seam allowances are necessary.

- When piecing, always place pieces right sides together and match raw edges; pin if necessary.

- Chain piecing saves time and will usually result in more accurate piecing.

- Trim away points of seam allowances that extend beyond edges of sewn pieces.

SEWING STRIP SETS

When there are several strips to assemble into a strip set, first sew strips together into pairs, then sew pairs together to form strip set. To help avoid distortion, sew seams in opposite directions *(Fig. 4)*.

Fig. 4

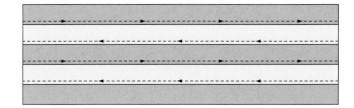

SEWING ACROSS SEAM INTERSECTIONS

When sewing across intersection of two seams, place pieces right sides together and match seams exactly, making sure seam allowances are pressed in opposite directions *(Fig. 5)*.

Fig. 5

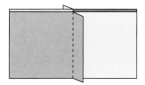

SEWING SHARP POINTS

To ensure sharp points when joining triangular or diagonal pieces, stitch across the center of the "X" (shown in pink) formed on wrong side by previous seams *(Fig. 6)*.

Fig. 6

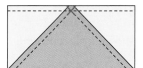

PRESSING

- Use steam iron set on "Cotton" for all pressing.

- Press after sewing each seam.

- Seam allowances are almost always pressed to one side, usually toward darker fabric. However, to reduce bulk it may occasionally be necessary to press seam allowances toward the lighter fabric or even to press them open.

- To prevent dark fabric seam allowance from showing through light fabric, trim darker seam allowance slightly narrower than lighter seam allowance.

- To press long seams, such as those in long strip sets, without curving or other distortion, lay strips across width of the ironing board.

- When sewing blocks into rows, seam allowances may be pressed in one direction in odd numbered rows and in the opposite direction in even numbered rows. When sewing rows together, press seam allowances in one direction.

QUILTING

Quilting holds the three layers (top, batting, and backing) of the quilt together and can be done by hand or machine. Because marking, layering, and quilting are interrelated and may be done in different orders depending on circumstances, please read entire **Quilting** *section, pages 44-45, before beginning project.*

MARKING QUILTING LINES

Quilting lines may be marked using fabric marking pencils, chalk markers, or water- or air-soluble pens.

Simple quilting designs may be marked with chalk or chalk pencil after basting. A small area may be marked, then quilted, before moving to next area to be marked. Intricate designs should be marked before basting using a more durable marker.

Caution: Pressing may permanently set some marks. **Test** different markers **on scrap fabric** to find one that marks clearly and can be thoroughly removed.

A wide variety of precut quilting stencils, as well as entire books of quilting patterns, are available. Using a stencil makes it easier to mark intricate or repetitive designs.

To make a stencil from a pattern, center template plastic over pattern and use a permanent marker to trace pattern onto plastic. Use a craft knife with single or double blade to cut channels along traced lines *(Fig. 7)*.

Fig. 7

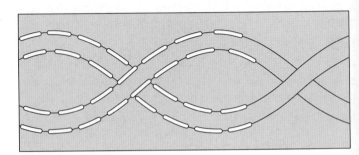

PREPARING THE BACKING

To allow for slight shifting of quilt top during quilting, backing should be approximately 4" larger on all sides. Yardage requirements listed for quilt backings are calculated for 43"/44"w fabric. Using 90"w or 108"w fabric for the backing of a bed-sized quilt may eliminate piecing. To piece a backing using 43"/44"w fabric, use the following instructions.

1. Measure length and width of quilt top; add 8" to each measurement.

2. If determined width is 79" or less, cut backing fabric into two lengths slightly longer than determined *length* measurement. Trim selvages. Place lengths with right sides facing and sew long edges together, forming tube *(Fig. 8)*. Match seams and press along one fold *(Fig. 9)*. Cut along pressed fold to form single piece *(Fig. 10)*.

| Fig. 8 | Fig. 9 | Fig. 10 |

3. If determined width is more than 79", it may require less fabric yardage if the backing is pieced horizontally. Divide determined *length* measurement by 40" to determine how many widths will be needed. Cut required number of widths the determined *width* measurement. Trim selvages. Sew long edges together to form single piece.

4. Trim backing to size determined in Step 1; press seam allowances open.

CHOOSING THE BATTING

The appropriate batting will make quilting easier. For fine hand quilting, choose low-loft batting. All cotton or cotton/polyester blend battings work well for machine quilting because the cotton helps "grip" quilt layers. If quilt is to be tied, a high-loft batting, sometimes called extra-loft or fat batting, may be used to make quilt "fluffy."

Types of batting include cotton, polyester, wool, cotton/polyester blend, cotton/wool blend, and silk.

When selecting batting, refer to package labels for characteristics and care instructions. Cut batting same size as prepared backing.

ASSEMBLING THE QUILT

- Examine wrong side of quilt top closely; trim any seam allowances and clip any threads that may show through front of the quilt. Press quilt top, being careful not to "set" any marked quilting lines.
- Place backing *wrong* side up on flat surface. Use masking tape to tape edges of backing to surface. Place batting on top of backing fabric. Smooth batting gently, being careful not to stretch or tear. Center quilt top *right* side up on batting.
- Use 1" rustproof safety pins to "pin-baste" all layers together, spacing pins approximately 4" apart. Begin at center and work toward outer edges to secure all layers. If possible, place pins away from areas that will be quilted, although pins may be removed as needed when quilting.

MACHINE QUILTING METHODS

Use general-purpose thread in bobbin. Do not use quilting thread. Thread the needle of machine with general-purpose thread or transparent monofilament thread to make quilting blend with quilt top fabrics. Use decorative thread, such as a metallic or contrasting-color general-purpose thread, to make quilting lines stand out more.

Straight-Line Quilting
The term "straight-line" is somewhat deceptive, since curves (especially gentle ones) as well as straight lines can be stitched with this technique.

1. Set stitch length for six to ten stitches per inch and attach walking foot to sewing machine.

2. Determine which section of quilt will have longest continuous quilting line, oftentimes area from center top to center bottom. Roll up and secure each edge of quilt to help reduce the bulk, keeping fabrics smooth. Smaller projects may not need to be rolled.

3. Begin stitching on longest quilting line, using very short stitches for the first 1/4" to "lock" quilting. Stitch across project, using one hand on each side of walking foot to slightly spread fabric and to guide fabric through machine. Lock stitches at end of quilting line.

4. Continue machine quilting, stitching longer quilting lines first to stabilize quilt before moving on to other areas.

Free-Motion Quilting
Free-motion quilting may be free form or may follow a marked pattern.

1. Attach darning foot to sewing machine and lower or cover feed dogs.

2. Position quilt under darning foot; lower foot. Holding top thread, take a stitch and pull bobbin thread to top of quilt. To "lock" beginning of quilting line, hold top and bobbin threads while making three to five stitches in place.

3. Use one hand on each side of darning foot to slightly spread fabric and to move fabric through the machine. Even stitch length is achieved by using smooth, flowing hand motion and steady machine speed. Slow machine speed and fast hand movement will create long stitches. Fast machine speed and slow hand movement will create short stitches. Move quilt sideways, back and forth, in a circular motion, or in a random motion to create desired designs; do not rotate quilt. Lock stitches at end of each quilting line.

MAKING A HANGING SLEEVE

Attaching a hanging sleeve to back of wall hanging or quilt before the binding is added allows project to be displayed on wall.

1. Measure width of quilt top edge and subtract 1". Cut piece of fabric 7"w by determined measurement.
2. Press short edges of fabric piece $1/4$" to wrong side; press edges $1/4$" to wrong side again and machine stitch in place.
3. Matching wrong sides, fold piece in half lengthwise to form tube.
4. Follow project instructions to sew binding to quilt top and to trim backing and batting. Before Blindstitching binding to backing, match raw edges and stitch hanging sleeve to center top edge on back of quilt.
5. Finish binding quilt, treating hanging sleeve as part of backing.
6. Blindstitch bottom of hanging sleeve to backing, taking care not to stitch through to front of quilt.
7. Insert dowel or slat into hanging sleeve.

BINDING

Binding encloses the raw edges of quilt. Because of its stretchiness, bias binding works well for binding projects with curves or rounded corners and tends to lie smooth and flat in any given circumstance. Binding may also be cut from straight lengthwise or crosswise grain of fabric.

MAKING STRAIGHT-GRAIN BINDING

1. To determine length of strip needed if attaching binding with mitered corners, measure edges of quilt and add 12".
2. To determine lengths of strips needed if attaching binding with overlapped corners, measure each edge of quilt; add 3" to each measurement.
3. Cut lengthwise or crosswise strips of binding fabric the determined length and the width called for in project instructions. Strips may be pieced to achieve necessary length.
4. Matching wrong sides and raw edges, press strip(s) in half lengthwise to complete binding.

ATTACHING BINDING WITH MITERED CORNERS

1. Beginning with one end near center on bottom edge of quilt, lay binding around quilt to make sure that seams in binding will not end up at a corner. Adjust placement if necessary. Matching raw edges of binding to raw edge of quilt top, pin binding to right side of quilt along one edge.

2. When you reach first corner, mark $1/4$" from corner of quilt top *(Fig. 11)*.

Fig. 11

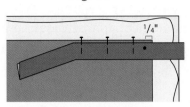

3. Beginning approximately 10" from end of binding and using $1/4$" seam allowance, sew binding to quilt, backstitching at beginning of stitching and at mark *(Fig. 12)*. Lift needle out of fabric and clip thread.

Fig. 12

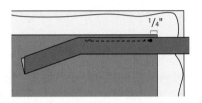

4. Fold binding as shown in *Figs. 13-14* and pin binding to adjacent side, matching raw edges. When you've reached the next corner, mark $1/4$" from edge of quilt top.

Fig. 13   Fig. 14

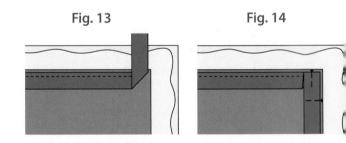

5. Backstitching at edge of quilt top, sew pinned bindin to quilt *(Fig. 15)*; backstitch at the next mark. Lift needle out of fabric and clip thread.

Fig. 15

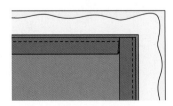

6. Continue sewing binding to quilt, stopping approximately 10" from starting point *(Fig. 16)*.

Fig. 16

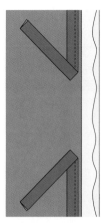

7. Bring beginning and end of binding to center of opening and fold each end back, leaving a ¹⁄₄" space between folds *(Fig. 17)*. Finger press folds.

Fig. 17

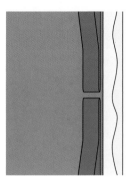

8. Unfold ends of binding and draw a line across wrong side in finger-pressed crease. Draw a line through the lengthwise pressed fold of binding at the same spot to create a cross mark. With edge of ruler at cross mark, line up 45° angle marking on ruler with one long side of binding. Draw a diagonal line from edge to edge. Repeat on remaining end, making sure that the two diagonal lines are angled the same way *(Fig. 18)*.

Fig. 18

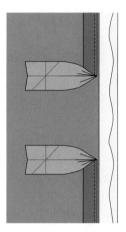

9. Matching right sides and diagonal lines, pin binding ends together at right angles *(Fig. 19)*.

Fig. 19

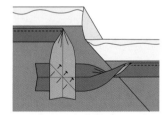

10. Machine stitch along diagonal line *(Fig. 20)*, removing pins as you stitch.

Fig. 20

11. Lay binding against quilt to double check that it is correct length.

12. Trim binding ends, leaving ¼" seam allowance; press seam open. Stitch binding to quilt.

13. If using 2½"w binding (finished size ½"), trim backing and batting a scant ¼" larger than quilt top so that batting and backing will fill the binding when it is folded over to quilt backing. If using narrower binding, trim backing and batting even with edges of quilt top.

14. On one edge of quilt, fold binding over to quilt backing and pin pressed edge in place, covering stitching line *(Fig. 21)*. On adjacent side, fold binding over, forming a mitered corner *(Fig. 22)*. Repeat to pin remainder of binding in place.

Fig. 21   Fig. 22

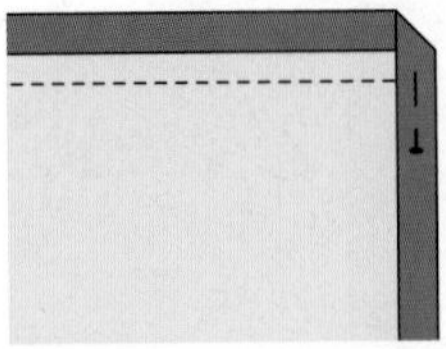

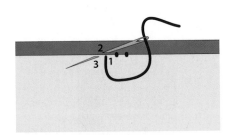

15. Blindstitch binding to backing *(Fig. 23)*, taking care not to stitch through to front of quilt.

Fig. 23